Financial Freedom

11 Steps to Financial Freedom

Table of Contents

INTRODUCTION

Congratulations on downloading this book and thank you for doing so.

The following chapters will discuss everything that you need to know in order to gain your own financial freedom. There are so many people in America who are dealing with issues of debt and never being able to get ahead. They want to finally get rid of their debt, but they are stuck in an endless cycle that will not let them go. They want to get rid of that debt today, but don't realize that while it was easy to get the debt, it does take some time to get rid of it. This guidebook is going to take some time to talk about how you can gain your financial freedom.

There are so many things that you are able to do when it comes to gaining your own financial freedom. This guidebook will take some time to discuss many topics such as what financial freedom is, what a passive income is and how you can earn one for yourself, and even how to invest your money and get it to work for you. In addition, we will talk about the eleven steps that you are able to take to finally reach your own financial freedom.

If you would like to reach financial freedom, it is important that you come up with a plan for success. This guidebook will take the time to help you learn how to gain financial freedom in no time!

There are plenty of books on this subject on the market, thanks again for choosing this one! Every effort was made to ensure it is full of as much useful information as possible, please enjoy!

CHAPTER 1

WHAT IS FINANCIAL FREEDOM?

While there are many things that you may dream to accomplish in your life, you will find that almost everyone is interested in gaining financial freedom. Being free financially means that you are able to maintain the lifestyle that you want without a regular paycheck. It is like having a retirement where you are able to live comfortably and maybe go out and have some fun without having to worry about stretching yourself too thin.

There are actually a lot of stages that come with gaining financial freedom. It is not really a single point in time, but rather four stages that will lead you to this. The four stages of financial freedom that you should follow include:

No freedom

Everyone is going to start out the journey at the same place. During this stage, you will rely on your monthly paycheck. You will see that a job as well as the reliable income stream that it provides is required so that you are able to pay the bills. If something happened to your income and you no longer received that paycheck, your savings would be depleted quickly, and you may end up defaulting on our monthly expenses. This is not the best place to be financially, but it is the starting point and you will be able to work from here.

Temporary freedom

In this second stage, you will still need your income on a regular basis, but you are able to spend less than what you earn. You can then turn the extra over into a pool of savings. You want to get into this stage so that you can build up a good savings, otherwise, you will end up with working forever because your lifestyle will depend on all the money that you earn. As you start to save some of your income, even if that amount is small in the beginning, you may want to consider investing your savings into a diversified investment that will provide you with a stream of income when it grows. Or, you have the possibility of starting a business on the side so that you can create a second source of income.

You will find that your freedom is going to grow along with your savings. Over time, you will have saved enough money so that you are comfortable. You may decide to take some time to travel for a year, go back to school, start your own business, switch jobs or do other things that would be hard if you worked a full-time job. These are big changes in your life, but these are not permanent changes. The freedom that comes with this stage is going to be temporary. Your income will usually exceed your expenses with this one and you will not be able to remain free for too long.

Permanent freedom

When you get to the third stage, the non-employment income that you make will be higher than what your total expenses are. You would be able to quit working your regular job and still have enough from your business or your investment that you are still able to pay all your bills. You should have a reliable income that keeps coming in so that you are able to enjoy life and gain a permanent freedom, not one that will be gone quickly.

Yes, if you have a side business, you are still going to put in some labor to make it work. You will still be trading your time for money. But it is much different compared to what you would do working for someone else. The side job that you take over should represent your passion and be something that you really enjoy doing. This means that while you may be working at a side job, you will enjoy it and you will feel like you are free.

Having fulfillment is the entire point of financial freedom. Just because you have freedom in this matter does not mean that you have to retire completely, unless you choose to. It's all about having independence to choose how your daily routine is going to go and it will allow you to design a better life while being able to spend your energy, money, and time in a way that is more meaningful. This could include investing, starting a side business, or doing something else that you enjoy that brings in money.

Luxurious freedom

This is a stage that is not going to be achieved by very many people. This is where you are able to have enough of a passive income that you are able to spend it freely. Your income is going to exceed the expenses that you have by a large margin so that you are able to live the lifestyle that you would like without having to put in much more work.

This one is going to take some time to accomplish. You will have to work hard at your passive income, and perhaps have a few different sources of this income, so that you can earn enough to make this work. You have a choice. You can choose to get your passive income to a point where you can cover the bills and then stop and hope you don't go backwards in the stages. Or you can work a bit longer and end up with the luxurious freedom that we just talked about.

Do you want financial freedom?

To start with this, there are three main questions that you should ask yourself. These include:

- Are you happy with the lifestyle that you have right now?

- Have you found a job that has a good work to life balance?

- Do you enjoy the job that you do and enjoy the purpose of your daily routine?

These are hard questions that you have to answer, but they will help you to determine what your thoughts are about gaining financial freedom. There are three categories that you can split these into. First, you have to check whether your work is meaningful. There are some individuals who like their jobs and who see no reason why they should stop working. This is just fine because you are able to work while also being financially free.

The second category is that work is okay for you. You do not particularly enjoy the job, but it is something that you do because it is something that you don't completely despise, which will pay the bills. You will have some good days and bad days, but you are pretty neutral about the job.

If you are in this second situation, your preferred level of freedom financially should be inversely related to the amount of disdain that you have for your work. It is up to you to work harder to increase the amount of savings that you have so that you can have more control and even change careers if you would like.

And finally, you could fall into the third group where you find work to be boring and somewhat terrible. For this group, financial freedom should be really high on your priority list. If you really hate the job you are in, it should be easy to make sacrifices to find a way to escape. This would include working a second job, moving somewhere that has a lower cost of living, and cutting out the unnecessary expenses. You should spend this time saving all the money that you can so that you are able to change jobs.

By focusing on this freedom, the perspective that you have is likely to change. You will go from sludging through many more years at a job you don't like to designing the life that you would like to have. If you put your mind to it, you will be able to devote all your energy, time, and money to that goal, and you are more likely to see success.

During this point, time, rather than money, is the most valuable asset that you have. If your time at that job is making you miserable, it is time to save money so that you can quit your job.

When it comes to financial freedom, you are the one who has to decide that it is something you want. It does take some hard work and some risks and not everyone is going to be able to handle this. But when you look at all the benefits that you get out of this freedom, it is going to become your biggest goal in no time.

CHAPTER 2

WHAT IS A PASSIVE INCOME?

One way that you can make sure that you are able to earn your financial freedom is to start looking at a passive income. This income is going to require some work on your part, and it does take some time to build up to the amount that you would like. But if you are successful, it can generate a lot of income while you get to do the things that you like. Let's spend some time in this chapter looking at what a passive income is and why it is so important to helping you earn your own financial freedom.

The first thing that we need to take a look at is what passive income is. This is some kind of earnings that you will get from a business, rental properties, limited partnerships, or other enterprises where you are not actively involved in the work. It is a form of income that will be taxable just like with active income, however, the IRS will treat it differently. In addition, portfolio income is sometimes considered passive income by some specialists, so if you earn some income from interest and dividends, then you are earning a passive income.

Let's take a better look at this. There are three categories that come to play when we are talking about income. These include portfolio income, passive income, and active income. Active income is going to be the type that you will earn when you go to a regular job. If you have a boss and you are expected to show up at work each day and you earn a set amount no matter how hard you work, then you have an active income.

A portfolio income would be one that you earned based off your investments. This is sometimes considered a passive income, but others will put it in its own category. If you have some money in the stock market or you are investing in another avenue, and you make money from these, then you will be able to have portfolio income.

With passive income, you are able to earn an income without being actively involved in the work. This is a relatively new term that is loosely used to define any money that is being earned with little to no effort on the part of the one who is getting it. Those who work with passive incomes will be those who are your own boss or work from home individuals. There are a lot of people who would have jobs that fit into this category. If you own real estate and have a property manager, have retirement pay, interest gains in stocks, and capital gains, you may have passive income.

One thing to remember is that while the activities above are going to fit the popular definition of what you see as passive income, they will not fit with the technical definition that the IRS has outlined. When we are talking about passive income from the viewpoint of the IRS, it is defined as either net rental income or income that comes from a business in which the taxpayer is not materially participating in. There are also some cases that will include interest that is self-charged.

Passive income and self-charged interest

When there is money that is lent over to an S-corporation or partnership acting as the pass-through entity, by that entity's owner, the interest income on that loan to the portfolio loan will often count as a form of passive income. This is going to count as passive income when you are dealing with the IRS.

Passive income and property

One big source of passive income for most people will be rental properties. These are usually going to be defined as a form of passive income, although there are a few exceptions. If you are considered a professional in real estate, any income that you make from rentals will be counted as active income. If you are doing what is known as self-renting, which means that you own a space and then you rent it out to a partnership or a corporation where you are conducting business, this will not count as a form of passive income unless you signed the lease before 1988. If the lease was signed before 1988, you were grandfathered into having an income that is passive.

However, if you have an income that comes from leasing land, this is not going to qualify as a form of passive income. This does not mean that you as a land owner will not be able to benefit from some of the passive income loss rules if that particular property nets a loss during any type of tax year. If you are just holding onto the land as a form of investing, any earnings would be under the active income category.

The no material participation

To have a passive income, you need to make sure that you are not materially participating in the whole process. When you start participating in the running of the company, you will turn it into an active income. You are able to invest in the company and make some profit from it, but you can't be there running it from day to day and still call it a passive income.

As an investor, you could add in $300,000 to a candy store and you come up with an agreement with the owner that you will earn a percentage of the earnings each year, then this would be a passive income. You will keep earning that profit, but as long as you do not participate in running the business at all, then it is a passive income.

However, if you do start to help manage the company along with the owners, then you are going to be seen as an active participant and your income then becomes active. This is because you are now helping out with material participation. There are a few rules that the IRS has in place when it comes to material participation and what counts as this for tax purposes. This includes:

- If you spend over 500 hours helping out or participating in a business or another activity that you are profiting from, it will be considered material participation.

- If the participation that you provide in an activity is substantially all of the participation that occurs for that year, it would be called material participation.

- If you participate in the activity for up to 100 hours, and that is equal to what other people do with that activity, then it is considered material participation.

You will have to be careful about how much time you are helping out with the business. If you spend too much time helping out with the business, it is going to be turned into an active income and it will be treated differently when it comes to the taxes that you pay.

What are the benefits of a passive income?

There are a lot of benefits that come with working with a passive income. First, you will be able to make an income without having to worry about working all the time. You will need to put some work in at the beginning to get things up and running. For example, to get started with a passive income in rental properties, you will need to put in the work to save up money to purchase the properties and then to maintain them until you make enough money. After you get a few properties and start making some good income, you can hire a property manager and spend very little time on this income source.

Think of all the free time that you can receive after all of this. You will need to put in all the hard work, but some of the good passive income sources that you can go with can make some good money for you. This allows you to make the money that you would like and still have free time on the side. You can go out with family and friends, travel the world, or even start up a second passive income. There is nothing better than the financial freedom that you will be able to get with a good passive income, and all the freedom of time that you get is not a bad thing either.

Grouping activities and passive income

If you would like to be able to save some effort and time, you are also able to group two, and sometimes more, passive activities, into one big activity. This works the best as long as these activities go together well. When you do this as a taxpayer, you will not need to provide material participation for each activity but can just do it for the activity as a whole.

The point of doing this is pretty simple to work with. If the activities are similar in terms of the type of business, or if they are interdependent in some way, then they will have the same customers, employees, or will use one type of book for accounting. This is basically going to make it easier for you to get several forms of passive income at once without all the work or taking up as much time.

Now, let's take a better look at how this is going to work. Let's say that you would like to own a sneaker store and a pretzel store that are located in malls in two different places. There are four options that you can use in order to group these passive income sources, including:

- Grouped into one activity. This can be done because all of the businesses are found in shopping malls.

- Grouped by their geography

- Grouped by the business type that you are working with. This would include retail sales since you are working with shoes and pretzels.

- Keep them ungrouped

Passive income is one of the best things that you can do for yourself if you want to make sure that you get the financial freedom that you want. These incomes take some hard work to get going, but once you do, you will be able to make a reliable source of income without much work at all.

Ideas for passive income

At this point, a passive income is probably sounding like a great deal. Who wouldn't want to earn an income without hardly needing to work at all. But what options do you have when it comes to finding the right passive income that helps you to earn a good amount of money, keeps the risks down, and so much more. Here are some of the options that you are able to work with in order to earn a passive income:

- Sell an eBook

- Create a blog and get some affiliate links on it

- Sell physical products online

- Find good ways to invest

- Create your own online course with a membership

- Create a comparison site

- Vending machines, laundromats, and game machines

- Work with a rental property

- Create a new YouTube channel and get advertising

- Re-sell online products and services

- Become a writer

- Create your own app or software

- Purchase and then rent out tools and equipment that are expensive

- Make a website for writing book reviews

- Become a digital publisher

- Try out peer-to-peer lending

- Create and then sell your own products

- Buy a business that is already existing and doing well online

- Sell things on eBay

- Become a silent partner in a real-world business (will need to have enough money to do this first)

- Sell merchandise and other things on your blog

- Purchase domain names and then resell them

- Create a video or a podcast that is based on interviews with experts

There are a lot of great ideas that you are able to work with when it comes to creating your own passive income, as long as you are able to pick out an income source that will provide you with money on a regular basis without making you put in a lot of work in the process.

CHAPTER 3

HOW TO INVEST YOUR MONEY TO MAKE MORE MONEY

Another way that you are able to earn money and gain your own financial freedom is for you to invest your money. Investing will allow you to grow your money over time because you are able to compound the returns. Compounding is a great thing when it comes to seeing your money grow. Thanks to this, you will be able to see a few dollars grow into millions of dollars, as long as you give it enough time. And the more money that you are able to invest, the more you will be able to earn from this compounding.

You may be worried about investing, it is actually a really good thing to do to grow your money. Sure, there is the risk that you will end up with a loss, but there is a lot of potential when it comes to getting a serious gain. Doing anything for the first time will seem terrifying, especially when we are talking about your money, but with some solid advice, you will be able to get this to work out well for you. Let's take a look at investing and how you will be able to use this for your needs.

Investing as a beginner

Investing is something that people are going to have a strong opinion about. There are also a lot of different trains of thought that come with it. Some of the different options that you may run across include the following:

- The doomsday preppers: With this category, people are sure that the financial system is going to collapse. They are going to choose to invest in the market, but all of their money will go with real estate or gold because they do not think any of the others will do well.

- The gambling day traders: These individuals are going to be the ones that you would be able to see in movies. They will always watch a computer screen or the television, checking at all times whether the market is changing in the right direction for them to see a profit.

- The indexers: These traders are going to be the ones who will invest in everything so that they are able to take all the advantage of the slow and steady increase in the overall value of the markets.

If you are already in one of the camps that are above, you may need to change your perspective. With trading, it is important to keep an open mind and learn some of the different strategies so that you are really able to earn money and do well with investments.

Considering the risk to the reward

Yes, no matter what kind of investment you choose to do, there is going to be some risk that comes with it. But the good news is there are some options that you are able to work with in order to lower the risk. If you choose to go with some options like day trading and penny stocks they are going to be really high in risk. But if you would like to turn this into a viable passive income to help with your financial freedom, then those are not the two options that you should choose to go with.

It is much better to go with a safer option such as an established company or working for the long-term with your retirement, in order to get the results that you would like. You will be able to earn a good amount of income from this, without holding onto as much risk. Though there will be times when you will be able to make more money with some of the risky options, you could also lose a lot of money, and you will need to spend a ton of time on them, so they are not the best options to go with.

What should I invest in?

There are a ton of great options that you can go with when it comes to investing your money to make you a good income. It is important that you are able to find a good balance between the amount of work you have to put in, the amount of money that you will be able to earn, and the amount of risk that comes with it. Some of the options that you can go with include:

Mutual funds

Mutual funds are a professionally managed investment. Your money is going to be pooled together with that from other investors. The fund managers will then take all that money and use it to purchase securities for the whole group. This is a good one to go with when you are just getting started and you are not able to put a ton of money towards the investment and it is usually a low risk option. Mutual fund will also allow you to invest in a large portfolio with lots of bonds and stocks, using one transaction, rather than taking up your time doing them all on your own.

There are a number of benefits that come with working on mutual funds. They are safer than other investments because they are diversified, and they will cost less than other investments. You will either pay just one trading commission, and sometimes you will not have to pay anything, compared to paying for dozens of commissions if you did it the traditional way. Your financial advisor will be able to help you make the purchase of these mutual funds when you are ready.

Working with retirement accounts

It is also possible to invest in your retirement account. This is a long-term investment that you can go with that is usually profitable because you are giving the market some time to grow. There are a number of options to go with when working on this one. If you are able to get a retirement plan through work, it is a good idea to go with a 401k. This allows you to get a matching contribution from your employer and you will not have to pay taxes on this money in the year that you put it in. However, when you take the money out of the account, you will need to pay taxes on the amount you added in as well as all the compound interest that you earned as well.

Another option is an IRA. This is an account that you can work on by yourself. You will not be able to earn a tax break in the year that you add money to the account. But it can still be beneficial because you are able to take the money out, including the money that you added in and the money that you earned in compound interest, without having to pay any taxes at all.

Individual stocks

It is also possible that you can do an investment of individual stocks. If you decide to go with this option, it is best to go with the slow and steady approach. It is best to never have more than ten percent of your portfolio in these individual stocks, at least not until you are comfortable and knowledgeable about what you are doing in the market.

A good place to start with stocks is to go with value investing. You should study this a little bit ahead of time, but it is basically where you are going to focus on heavy amounts of research and then rely on the buy and hold mentality with your stocks.

Real estate

You can also work with real estate. There are a lot of different options that you are able to work with when it comes to real estate and the option that you go with is going to depend on the end results that you would like to get. The first option that some people will go with is to purchase a property and then fix it up before re-selling it.

This will take some time and some swat equity. You must be able to find some good homes that do not require a lot of work on your part but are available at a good deal. You also need to be quick at the work because the sooner you are able to sell the home after the purchase, the more money you will make.

You can also go with renting out a property. This works similar to the process above, but you will choose to keep the property and have tenants live inside and pay rent. This works well in several ways. You will get the tenant to pay off your mortgage so that you are able to build equity, which can help you in the long run, whether or not you ever sell the property. You will also be able to charge a rent that provides you with some extra cash each month. Add a few buildings into your portfolio and you will make some good money.

You can also work with selling contracts. These do not require you to actually own the property. You will simply go through and make a deal on a home that is in good shape but is at a discount. You can then find other investors who are looking for these kinds of properties and who are wiling to pay you for the contract. This basically requires you to do the legwork and if you do it right, you will never have to put much money into it or actually own the property.

Crowdfunding

Another investment option that you are able to go with is crowdfunding. You will be able to work with a variety of websites to get this done such as Fundrise and EquityMultiple in order to invest with as little as $1000. There are a lot of options when it comes to investing in crowdfunding. You can work with peer to peer ventures, real estate, and more. You need to be careful with who you are lending out money to though, or you will end up losing it all.

Cryptocurrencies

Another type of investing that has started to take over and is making a lot of people rich is investing in digital currencies. Bitcoin and some of the others on the market are making a big splash and this could be a great way to bring in some money with investing, as long as you know what you are doing. This is not something to get into if you are just starting with investing or something that you choose just because everyone else is doing it. This is a hard process to work with and since it is a new market, it is sometimes hard to know where it will go in the future.

With that being said, there are some options that you can go with when working in cryptocurrencies and you can make a lot of money. If you are a beginner and don't know much about this investment, it is probably best to stay away from day trading and some of the other riskier investment options. A good one to go with is the buy and hold strategy because it requires very little work and can potentially make you a lot of money without trying hard.

With the buy and hold strategy, you will simply purchase some of the digital currency that you want to work with. Then you store it in a wallet that is secure until sometime in the future. You will have to watch the market to make sure that the currencies don't go down. Most of these are on a steady rise up, but since there is not a lot of long-term data about them, it is hard to know how the currencies will do in the future. But if the market goes up, you could easily make a big profit without having to do much more other than check up on the market each day.

As you can see here, there are a lot of different things that you are able to do in order to properly invest your money. Investing your money may seem like it is a lot of work, but it is actually a really good way to ensure that you are making money, and perhaps a passive income, without having to work for a boss any longer. Make sure to check out these ideas and pick out which investment option is the right one for you.

CHAPTER 4

YOUR 11 STEPS TO
FINANCIAL FREEDOM

Financial freedom is something that all of us would like to reach some day. You may dream of the day when you will be able to pay off that last bill and not have to worry so much about all your checks going to debts. Think about how it will feel to finally make those debts go away and how it will feel to be able to spend your money the way that you want, rather than sending all your money to your creditors.

This financial freedom is a dream that most people have, but they often do not know what they need to do to get to that point. There is a lot of work that goes into earning your financial freedom and it is not something that is going to occur overnight. But if you are willing to work for it and try to stick with a budget to see success, then you will find that it is something that is within your reach.

With that being said, there are a number of things that you will need to accomplish before you will reach financial freedom. Some of the things that you will need to do include the following eleven steps:

Figure out which debts you owe

It is impossible to know what you need to take care of and to gain financial freedom if you have no idea how much you owe in debts. Most Americans are paying a little bit of their debts off each month, but a lot of these payments are set to automatic and they will never take the time to look at how much they owe. And with minimum payments and high interest rates, it is likely that you owe more than you think.

To help you get started with a budget that will help you to reach your own financial freedom, you need to take some time to look through your debts and get a good idea of how much you owe. Go through and find out who owns your debts and then write down how much you owe in each one. You may also want to write down more information about the debt, such as who owns it, how much you owe, what the minimum payment is, the interest and fees that you owe, and when that loan is due to be paid off.

Once you have this information in place, it is time to calculate how much you owe. This is often going to cause a little bit of sticker price when it comes to the amount that you owe. But this is still a good thing. This allows you to see how much you owe and will maybe be the motivation that you need to finally turn it all around.

If you are unsure about all the debts you owe, it is time to make some changes. It is never a good sign to not know how much you owe to others at any given time. A good way to figure out how much you owe is to go look at your credit report. There are three major credit reporting bureaus in the country. They figure out your credit score a little bit differently for each one, but the information that is on your credit report should be the same for each one. You are also allowed to get a free copy of that credit report from each agency once a year. Now is the time to print off one of the credit reports and see where all your debts are. While you are at it, make sure to check whether all the debts are legitimate or if you need to ask for some changes. Consider splitting up the credit reports so you can look at them at different times of the year without having to pay.

Talk with your spouse about your financial goals

It is important that you and your spouse are on the same page when it comes to creating a good financial plan. It does not make much sense for you to work so hard a creating a budget and trying to stick with it if your spouse is still going out and splurging on the money that you are trying to save. You both need to be in this together in order to make it all work.

A good thing to do is to include your spouse in this whole process. You should first sit down and take some time to discuss the goals that you have when it comes to money. Would you like to get all your debts paid down? Would you like to be able to save up for retirement, college, or something else? Would you like o be able to go on more vacations in the future? Each couple is going to have different financial goals, but the important thing is that you and your spouse need to talk about these goals and come up with a plan together.

In addition, you should both take a look at the budget together. This will help both of you to see where you are and how far you need to go to reach your goals. There is just something about looking at the budget that makes it easier to figure out how much you are spending and how much you will be able to cut back to make those goals. These goals can take some time to achieve, but when you and your spouse are on the same page, it becomes so much easier to reach them compared to doing this all on your own.

You both need to be willing to be honest about your financial goals and where you would like to end up in the future in terms of your finances. You also may both need to make some compromises to ensure that you will get there. If your husband has to give up their monthly gym membership and just work out at home, then you may need to give up your weekly time at the nail salon or something else that is a splurge to you. This is hard, but it is much easier when both parties work together rather than letting one person take over all the sacrifice.

Create a budget on your income, not your debts

Creating a budget is so important if you are working on gaining your financial freedom. This helps you to know how much money is coming in and how much is going out and will give you a good idea on the things that you will need to change in your financial world. But the trick here is that you need to create a budget that is based on the amount of money that you are bringing in, rather than basing one off the debts that you have. Yes, you will use your budget to help pay off your debts, but you need to allocate the funds that you have rather than worrying about how much you owe in other areas.

Working on this budget does not have to be too difficult. The first thing that you need to do is collect information on all the income that you are bringing in each month. This can include your income, your spouse's income, any investments that you own, rental properties, and more. If it is a regular source of income that you can rely on, then count it as your income. Write this number at the top of your paper.

Next, you need to go through and figure out how much debt you have and how much you will need to spend to make the minimum payments. You can also go through and see what all you spend on, even if that amount is not a debt, to help you see where your money is going. This can include the splurges that you spend on, groceries, internet, and more. Write this number down.

If your income number is higher than what you spend, then you are already doing a great job with the budgeting that you do. But if you are like most people, you are spending more than you earn and you may be putting the extra on a credit card or not paying your debts. If tis sounds like you, then it is time to go through and create a good budget.

There are a few things that you are able to do here. First, you should figure out spots where you are able to cut things out. Do you really need to spend $100 on your hair each month, pay for an expensive cable package that you never watch, or go out as often as you do? There are always ways that you are able to cut down on your spending and the more that you are able to do this, the more you will be able to put towards paying off your debts.

While you are working on this budget, it is important to save a spot to deal with the savings that you want to use. It is always a good idea to have at least a little bit of money in your savings account so while you go through this budget, take the time to start a savings account to make it easier to put money back for when you need it.

There are a lot of great programs, apps, and other resources that you can use that will make it easier for you to create a budget. This is something that is so important for everyone to do, and it could be a real eye opener as well. You may be surprised at how much you are paying on interest and other fees when you are working on your debts. If you are someone who is living paycheck to paycheck, you may be surprised that you would be able to put some money back into savings if you just cut out a few extras from your spending. No matter who you are, it is time to get serious about your spending and a budget will make this easier to handle.

Always track your spending

One thing that a lot of people have trouble with is tracking their spending. They have all the best ideas of what they want to do with their spending and their budget, but then they get to the end of the month and find out that they went over their limits and now they are no better than they were before. This can be frustrating, but the most likely culprit is that they are not tracking their spending all that well. They end up spending a ton because they think they are within their budget, but at the end of the month, they find out that they were wrong.

If you get to the end of the month and you can't figure out where all your money keeps going, then it is time to be held accountable for your spending. There are a few steps that you can take to help you to track your own spending. These will include the following:

- Track by store: With all the mega stores that are out there now, it is sometimes hard to track of all the different categories of spending that you do. If you shop at Walmart or Target, it is hard to know how much you spent on clothing, food, games, and so on. Rather than doing the budgeting by category, why not budget by store? You can set up a limit for how much you are allowed to spend on the stores you frequent most. This makes it easier to keep track of how much you are spending when you go out.

- Have a separate account for spending: This is a good way to budget if you are lazy. You can have one account that you use to pay for your bills, including things that may not be due each month. You and your partner will set up how much you will place in that account each month and then the rest of the income will go into separate accounts that are used for spending. This helps both parties to know that the essentials are taken care of and the other account is the one you can spend out of. Once that money is gone, though, you are done with shopping for the month.

- Track as you go: If you are the only one who is spending or making the decisions on spending, then this may be the one to go with. You can take out a spreadsheet and then plot down all of your known bills while keeping a tally of your credit card balance, so you know where that is each month.

- Work with an app: There are many apps out there that are meant to help you budget, but one of the most popular ones is Mint.com. This will help you to keep track of your budget and get some personalizations on how to do better. You should research some of the options that are available for apps so that you can properly use them to track your spending.

- Use the envelop method: This is a great way to keep your budget in check and you are able to use it in any way that you would like. With this, you can organize it in any way that you would like. You can have envelopes to help with savings, one that is there in case the vehicle needs repaired at some point, for a new car or other purchase, and even to keep your grocery bill in check. You can go through and decide how to use the envelopes, but this method helps you to keep things in order.

No matter which method you choose to go with, it is important that you find some method that will help you to keep track of your spending so that more money stays in your pocket, rather than going to someone else or to your debts.

Start and emergency fund

It is always a good idea to have an emergency fund in case you have something happen. You never know when there will be something big that happens in your life and you will need to come up with some money to help cover it. Or you or someone else in your home will lose their job and you will need to have some way to keep paying the bills. This is where the emergency fund can come into play.

It is usually recommended that you have about three to six months of an emergency fund saved up to help you out in case something happens. This amount should be enough so that if you have something bad happen and you can't work or aren't making money, you will still be able to pay your bills and other requirements for at least three to six months.

If you are looking at your bills and feel that the three to six months is a huge amount that you will never be able to save up, do not fret. Having any kind of emergency fund is important and you are allowed to work up to that larger amount. If you are just starting out, it is fine to start out with a smaller number. Why not work with a $1000 emergency fund? At least this is something in the bank to help you out. And over time, and with some more savings, you will eventually get to that three to six months.

A good way to start your emergency fund is to set up an account and then have automatic payments get sent there each month. You can set the amount and let the banks do all the work for you. You do not even need to think about it again after you get it all set up. Once this is done, you will be able to see that your emergency fund and your savings are going to add up quickly without you needing to put in any effort.

Pay off your debts with the snowball method

The snowball method is one of the best options that you are able to work with when it comes to getting rid of those debts. It allows you to get those debts paid down without as much stress and it can actually be one of the fastest methods to use. By now, you should have a good budget in place to help you know which debts you owe and how much. You will be able to use this information to help you to work on the snowball method.

The first thing that you need to do is pay the minimum on all your debts each month. You should not ignore any of the debts to make this happen. After these are all set up, you will choose the bill that you would like to pay off first. Some people go with the biggest debt and others will choose to go with the debt that has the highest interest rate. Any money that you have extra at the end of the month will go to paying down that debt. Even an extra $20 a month will make a difference, but the more that you can put towards the loan, the better off you will be.

Once the first debt is paid off, you will pick out the next loan that you would like to pay off. While still paying the minimum on your other debts, you will go through and add the payment that you were making to the first debt to the second debt, along with any extra that you have each month as well. This keeps on going until all the debts are paid off. When one debt is done, you will take all the payments that you were making on the previous debts and start putting that amount towards the next debt in line. The first debt will often take a long time to complete, but once that is done, the process will go faster as you are able to put more and more money towards the debts that you owe.

This snowball method will make sure that you are at least keeping up with the minimum amount that you owe on all your debts, but it is also allowing you to pay down some extra each month. And since you have some visible points where you can watch the bills get paid down, it is a great motivator. Be prepared that the first debt will take the longest, but by the time you are able to put all that money towards the last debt, it will be paid off in no time.

After you are done paying off all your debts, take that money and either add it to a savings account, add it as extra to your own retirement plan, or use it as a way to invest. Work hard to not add in any more debt to your life so that you do not need to go through this process again.

Put 15 percent of your pretax income back for retirement

One thing that a lot of people do not think about is how they will plan for retirement. They have a lot of good plans for their budget and saving money, but they forget about saving for their retirement. But unless you want to keep working for the rest of your life, it is important to get a good retirement plan up and running as soon as possible.

It is often recommended that you save about 15 percent of your income before tax for your retirement. If you are able to save back more each year, then this is a good idea as well. You never know what is going to happen in the future, but most people wish to have a good retirement without worries or stress because they don't have money and have to go back to work. This 15 percent, started as early as possible, will ensure that you are able to get a good retirement going now.

Of course, you must make sure that you start as early as possible. Due to the wonders of compound interest, you will be able to make a lot more if you start in your 20s compared to waiting until your 30s or 40s. Not only will you be able to put more money into the account, but you will be able to earn (on average) between six and eight percent each year on the investment. That will quickly add up to a great retirement.

Now, if you do not have a retirement and you are already in your 30s or 40s, it is still a good idea to get started. Better late than never when it comes to your retirement, though you may want to consider adding a higher percentage in so that you can make up for lost time. When it comes to retirement though, the more that you are able to put away and the earlier you are able to start, the better off you will be during retirement.

You should sit down and discuss the different retirement options that are available for you with your financial advisor. They will be able to discuss which account you should open and what you should invest in to see the best results. In addition, if you are able to, it may be best to work with your employer's 401k because this allows you to get a match from your employer and that makes the retirement go up faster than before.

Save for the larger purchase you want

If you are like most Americans, you will take out that credit card or another loan when you want a new car, new appliances, or some other big purchase. But outside of purchasing your home, it is never a good idea to take out more debt to get the things that you want.

The first issue is that if you are taking out a loan or more debt to pay for the item, then you are not really able to afford it. It is much better to save up the money and pay for that item rather than taking on more debt and hoping that you will be able to pay it off down the road. By the time you have saved up the money to make the purchase, you should have a good idea of whether you really want the item and you can do the proper research on the item to see if it is right for you.

Another issue is that these new debts are going to increase the amount that you will owe on the items you purchase. If you use a loan to purchase a car, it may be that you ask for $3000, but you could end up paying $700 or more extra in interest over the next few years for that loan. This is good news for those who own the loan because they will make a profit, but bad news for you when you want to pay off your debts and save money.

It is even worse when you are dealing with credit card debt. While you may be able to get a good percentage for interest on a loan, the credit cards will usually be above 20 percent. This is going to add up quickly and that $3000 vehicle (or whatever other thing you purchased with the money) could easily double or more by the time you are able to pay it down.

So, when you learn how to save up for the items that you want, you are actually saving yourself a ton of money on the debt that you would incur. Sure, you will need to wait longer to get the item, but it will be well worth it in the long run.

Cut up the credit cards

Credit card spending is something that most individuals and families are dealing with. They may use these cards in an emergency or will treat them like cash and go out and spend way too much on them. When it comes time to pay, they owe more than they thought and then the interest and the yearly fees can make it all worse. Just paying the minimum on these (which is usually all that people are able to afford) can take years and will double the amount that you owe on the card.

It is tempting to bring out that card, even when you are working so hard to pay off debts and gain the financial freedom that you want. You may decide to splurge on something or use it for something that you do not really need. Instead of keeping these cards around and spending more money than you have, it is time to cut those cards up. You can keep them open to help pay the bills off and to ensure that you do not ruin your credit score, but when you slice up the cards, you can't use them at all and can concentrate on paying the balance off.

In addition, after you cut up those credit cards and get the balance paid down, do not sign up for some more. It is tempting to do this if you want to get the points or the other benefits of signing up for the card, but it is not worth it. And you have already proven that you can't be trusted when it comes to using credit cards smartly. If you are not careful, you will end up right back at the spot that you started at, and that can make it hard to start over again. Just stay away from credit cards and learn how to pay cash for the things that you need instead.

Pay off your mortgage early

After you have taken some time to pay off the rest of the debts that you owe, it is time to work on paying off that mortgage. While a mortgage is a debt, it is seen a little bit differently than a regular debt and so this is usually the last thing that you would want to worry about when paying things off. It is also one of the biggest debts so paying off the smaller ones is a much better idea.

Now that your other debts are paid off, it is time to start making extra payments on the mortgage. You should start making these as early as you can on the loan. Because you are working with mortgage payments that are amortized, most of the interest is going to be put on at the beginning. As you pay off the interest, you will start paying off more of the principal with each payment. If you own your home, you will notice that the first five years or so of payments will be mostly interest towards the loan. But if you are starting to make extra payments, you can get that interest paid down and will be more likely to pay it all off. Since you are done with paying your other bills, it should not be too hard to pay an extra payment each month to get that gone.

If you are not able to put a full payment extra towards your mortgage each month, there are still some other options to go with. Some people like to schedule it so that they send over a lump sum to the payment at the end of the year. You could take your tax return or a bonus from work and do this. Of course, double check and see if your mortgage charges a penalty for prepaying on the loan. Most will not do this, but it is always best to check.

For those who are only able to pay a little extra each month, that is fine. You can add a small amount to your mortgage payments each month. Even a little bit is going to make a big difference in how much you pay to the loan over the long term. This also makes it easier to budget the amount in each month.

You should keep track of your mortgage and look for some new refinancing benefits that come up. While this is a lengthy process and could get expensive if you are doing it all the time, it is something to consider. If you are someone who has a huge interest rate, it's maybe time to refinance and get that part lowered. This could save you thousands of dollars over the term of the loan and will make it easier to pay off.

There are a number of benefits that come with paying off your mortgage early. First, it will save you a lot of money when you are dealing with the interest that you owe. You could end up saving thousands of dollars in interest based on how much you pay off extra and how early you decide to start the process.

In addition, paying down more of the mortgage means that you will earn more equity in the property. This equity will help you out when you wish to sell the property for moving or if you would like to downsize and use that money to pay off more debts. The more equity that you have in the home, the more money you would be able to put into your pocket if you decide to sell it. It also can be used to help you get some more credit, but that is not a good idea to work with if you are trying to pay down debts and gain financial freedom.

And the best thing about paying off your mortgage early is that you will not have to pay that big bill each month. You will still be in charge of paying off your taxes and our insurance each month, but the major amount that you pay each month when it comes to your mortgage will disappear. Think of all the great things that you will be able to do when you open up that money.

Learn how to slash your taxes

While there are a lot of people who are worried about paying off their taxes because they think that these are too complicated, tax planning can be simple. There are a lot of different programs that you are able to use to make this happen and will ensure that you will be able to slash those taxes in no time. You are probably already doing a lot of the things that you should be already.

There are a lot of ways that you will be able to reduce the amount of taxes that you owe. Making sure that you take out the right amount out of your paycheck each pay period can help. Paying interest on your home or your student loans can help. Putting money into a retirement plan and not taking it out can help.

This may seem a bit overwhelming at the beginning. First, you should consider working with a tax accountant. They will be able to look over your income and your financial status and will hep you to know how to cut down the taxes and save as much as possible. You can always ask them any questions that you have, and they will be able to provide you with some suggestions on how you can cut down on your tax bill in the coming years.

If you have a low to a moderate income paying down your debt, and this will include paying down your mortgage, will be the best tax planning that you can do. This is because you then will not have to pay taxes on the capital gains that are on our home and there will be no taxes charged on your return for being out of debt. For those who are in the higher tax brackets, earning more than $85,000 a year, it is a good time to talk with an accountant and see what mix of investment options, such as TFSA's, RESPs, and RRSPs, would be the best for you to keep those taxes as low as possible.

There are a lot of ways that you will be able to cut down on those taxes. If you are paying off student loan debt, you will be able to write off the amount that you pay on interest each year. You can write off some of the interest that you pay on your home as well as the taxes. If you have children, this will provide you with a good tax reduction as well. If you purchase anything for your business to start a passive income, this can be counted in there as well. These are just some of the most common ways that you will be able to slash your taxes. Talking to a tax professional will help you to get as many tax deductions as you can so you can use that money in other ways.

As you can see, there are a lot of different things that you are able to do to help keep your debt as small as possible and to gain financial freedom. It does not matter how much money you earn; with the right financial planning and some hard work, you will be able to get your finance in check and gain that freedom that you have always dreamed about.

CONCLUSION

Thanks for making it through to the end of this book, let's hope it was informative and able to provide you with all of the tools you need to achieve your goals whatever they may be.

The next step is to take the advice that is in this guidebook and go through and follow the steps so that you can finally get the financial freedom that you are looking for. There are a lot of people who dream about the day when they will finally have that financial freedom, but they feel like they just have too many debts. But no matter how much debt you have, with some hard work and dedication, and a good plan, you will be able to get the results that you want.

This guidebook has all the tips that you need to help you gain that financial freedom. We will talk about what financial freedom means, how to invest your money, and even the eleven steps that you should take to finally get that financial freedom. It is important to know that there are a ton of ways that you will be able to pay off debts and keep your finances in order, but it is a process that will take some time. Do not get frustrated that you are not able to pay off everything really quickly. With the help of the tips in this guidebook, you will get there, it just takes time.

When you are tired of having to give all your money to someone else to pay off your debts and you want to finally get your finances in order, make sure to check out this guidebook to help you get started.

Finally, if you found this book useful in anyway, a review on Amazon is always appreciated!